Searching For Parker

The life and loves of a closet nympho

L. Penelope OAP

Publish & Print
www.publishandprint.co.uk

Front cover photograph by Adam Gonzales @adamgonzales

Illustrator: *'Dave'*

Dedicated to:

Kim who quite literally saved my life and my sanity during and since inserting my pacemaker; Mark who, with his taxi, has picked me up whenever I or the car have been indisposed. To my amazing lovely friends including Angela, Eileen, June, Lyn, Maryann, Mel, Mitch, Therese and Vanessa who made me smile and laugh over the bizarre, funny and often significant challenges we encountered; Sean who helped me to find a reason for writing this book; Sue and Dave for their sound advice and Tara and Drags who, somehow have managed to keep my hair looking good for around 12 and 25 years respectively. Last but not least the beautiful cats who have deigned to live with me – currently Boggins and Scramble. They too help to keep me sane and ensure that I'm never talking to myself or drinking alone.

Prologue

Let me say at the outset, I believe in lust at first sight and not love at first sight. Having lusted after numerous men, and engaged in mediocre sex, even riotous sex with a significant number, I can count the times I have been 'in love' *and* maintained the lust, in single figures.

This collection of musings is a result of a life lived well but not always wisely. One recent example that doesn't figure in the success stories is my one liaison with a Scandinavian. He was very tall, very large and totally uninhibited. We found each other online and met in a car park in broad daylight. Immediately after saying hello he tried to grope me. I laughed. He had a very vivid imagination and used to tell stories that beggared belief. When I'd refer to them at a later date he insisted that he'd never said such and such. Walter Mitty came to mind. Physically he wasn't my type but he was fascinating. He's travelled the world, flies his own plane, and has a good sense of humour. In bed he lacked finesse and, at times, it was like being shafted by a battering ram. On one occasion he must have masturbated before he came to me because he was taking forever. I'd had enough and decided to finish him off. My bum and associated parts went into jackhammer mode and he came very quickly with a loud roar. Apparently his legs felt like jelly. I was sore for days. He texts me every so often but I don't want any more of that.

Chapter 1

Early days

As a very small child I recall seeing a tall, white haired man in the garden with my pregnant mother. In my teens I discovered that my brother and I were illegitimate and my mother, a Catholic teacher and then headteacher, lived in fear of being found out. Apparently my father was a Belgian merchant seaman and had a family in Wales. I don't know if he was also my brother's father as we don't look alike and have very different personalities. My mother was on a massive guilt trip and the words, 'you'll go to hell if...', passed her lips frequently. She was always so stressed and worried about being found out and losing her job. Looking back I can empathise totally, I wish I had done so sooner. However I deeply resented her extreme efforts to keep me safe from a similar fate. It just made me desperate to find out what I was missing.

There was a constant focus on money. She was always overdrawn by next month's salary and she made all her clothes and mine too. I never wanted to find myself in a similar position. When I started work I can still remember the first item of clothing I bought – a purple, tight-fitting blouse. Unfortunately within a few months, I'd burnt a hole in one of the sleeves but by then it wasn't such a big deal.

Growing up, the first place I remember is a half way house on the Thames Embankment. I guess that's the equivalent of a refuge nowadays. At some point we moved to a prefab on the outskirts of south London. Then was a major move to the Midlands at which point our surname changed. I still have no idea why. After lodging in various places we finally got a small terraced council house. The loo was outside, there was no heating, and a tin bath hung behind the back door. In my early teens we moved to a council house on a new housing estate miles from anywhere. Next up was another council house, quite old but it did have an indoor loo and a bath. No shower, but much closer to town.

We never, ever had a conversation about sex. When I was around 7/8 years of age I discovered the joy of masturbation and I just knew there had to be more to it than that. When I was 11 years old my mother gave me a tiny Catholic book on reproduction. I'd already read it because I'd found it hidden away in a drawer. Neither my mother nor the book told me that my genitals would suddenly sprout hair and my inner labia would double in length almost overnight. I thought there was something wrong with me and was keen to compare my bits with my cousin and a girl I was friends with. The girl told her parents and the father came around to have a conversation with my mother. She still didn't say anything to me! I was just never allowed to see that girl alone again. I made do with my cousin and occasional explos with her in the girls' loo at the primary school where my mother taught. Nowadays that would probably be suspected peer on peer abuse. I don't deny that deliberate child on child abuse happens, but it is vital that Social Services investigate. Such activity may be a reaction to abuse within the family in which case the child, sometimes as young as 3, is a victim not a perpetrator. It is important not to jump to conclusions.

The first penis I saw was my brother's, when he was a baby and my mother was washing him. She used to roll back his foreskin, which I thought must be very painful. I worried terribly that the little knob at the end would fall off or out. When he was around 11 years old she had him circumcised, I didn't ask why. There was no doubt then that he was in pain. That was the limit of my knowledge of the male anatomy until some years later.

Until around the age of 16 any perceived transgressions were punished by a beating using a leather belt kept in the sideboard drawer. That only stopped when, one day, hunched on the floor, I willed myself not to cry. I just looked up at her. The beatings stopped. Another friend also from an Irish family said she'd had similar experiences. During my secondary schooling I had to take a lot of time off to look after my brother. He feigned illness to avoid the bullying at school. As far as I know nobody from my school checked why I was absent. Through sheer hard work I got ten good GCSEs, including Latin! That secured a place in college for the following year conditional on studying an A level. As an early autumn born child this was my chance to become the youngest in my year group.

A couple of years later I came home from college once and my brother was nowhere to be seen. My mother said she had thrashed him up the stairs to bed. When I got back to college I phoned the headteacher at his school and told him what was going on. I gather that, from that point on, he would call my brother into his room and ask if everything was alright. As we grew older we took different life paths and, several years ago had a major falling out. That rift is beyond repair.

My sexual encounters began very innocently, lusting after one of the 'naughty boys' in my primary school. There were lots of soulful glances across the playground but neither of us ever spoke. My mother would have gone ballistic at both of us. I didn't want to risk that.

Having passed the 11+ I went to an all girls, Catholic convent school. Had I been a bit more savvy I would have failed and gone to the local, mixed comprehensive school, but I am quite driven to succeed, a very Virgo, Virgo as an astrologer once told me. Not long after starting with the nuns I also learned that Convent educated girls are often 'gagging for it' and I totally understand why.

Then there was pudgy, pasty-faced Polish boy with curly hair who used to wait at the bus stop just up from mine. He never even noticed me and I was gutted. The next focus of my desire was a tall, thin red head that I soon discovered was determined to become a priest. I clearly had a lot to learn. Somewhere in the midst of all of this early lusting phase my mother took my brother and I to St Ives for a caravan holiday. That was bliss compared to previous holidays in the home of one of her siblings in Derry. My mother was one of 8 or 9 children and one of her sisters in Ireland took a similar path. Double beds had to hold up to 6 of us, head to feet. When we got home we had to go through ritual de-fleaing and de-lousing.

St Ives was where I really got started. We wandered into a daytime disco and I was asked to dance by a young man. When our thighs touched it was as though an electric bolt ran through my entire body. Who knows what would have happened had my mother and brother not been sitting less than 4 feet away, watching every move.

Somehow or other I got to go on a walk with a lovely lad from Dagenham, called Derek. On a rock above pounding waves I had my first kiss. I so wanted more.

My next encounter was in the public library. During school lunchtimes I started going to the library and there I met Alan. The attraction was immediate and the only place we could go for privacy was the top of the stairs behind the reference library. As often as possible we would meet and stick our tongues down each others' throats. I had no idea what else we might do even if we had the opportunity. I don't think he did either. It made concentrating in the afternoon a bit tricky.

My knowledge was enhanced when I caught the attention of one of the local football team stars. I must have been around 15 at the time, as flat as a plank, but he had decided to enlighten me about what to expect when I was older. So there was a fair bit of groping and kissing and then he told me about men kissing women 'down there'!!! I could not imagine how that might feel but I certainly wanted to find out.

Then came a man, aged late 30s that I met in the coffee shop. I was 16 at the time. I had no idea about contraception but I found out PDQ. I lost my virginity to him, a Jersey man who worked at the local swimming baths. After frantic tumbling in the back seat of his car, one night I found I was bleeding profusely. With hindsight I realised I had miscarried but, if my mother guessed, she didn't say and I stayed in bed till the bleeding stopped. Undeterred I then got involved with a 40+ male and we met in his bungalow. I wasn't allowed to stray from the lounge and I suspect he was possibly into pornography. Thank goodness it was pre-Internet days.

Next up was the footballer's older brother. His wife was a formidable character but she wasn't always around, so while mother was at work, and his wife was otherwise engaged, we would have sex in the kitchen. What killed that? When he came he shouted his wife's name!

Many, many years later I realised that what I had taken to be affection was child sexual abuse. Hindsight is a wonderful thing.

Happily I survived 'till college. The only way my mother would allow me to go was to a, guess what, a female only Catholic college run by nuns. The college doctor was a wise old bird and he put me on the pill 'because of my irregular periods'. Hurrah! Sexual freedom for the first time AND breasts appeared but sadly subsided within a matter of weeks.

When I accidentally left my make up bag behind, on a visit home, my mother found my pills and tipped up at the college, to get me thrown out. My friends hid me and the principal, a tall, very kindly and perceptive woman, met my mother and sent her away. The principal then became my de facto guardian. The age of majority in those days was 21. Hard to believe.

Despite the freedom afforded by the pill I led a fairly chaste existence, two relationships. The first was totally obsessive about appearances. I used to get my hair done every time before I went to his family home. He would still find a hair to pick off my jacket or some other 'blemish', when he picked me up from the station. His mother and father were fairly relaxed but still made him sleep downstairs which led to much tiptoeing around in the night. They occasionally would go out and leave us alone in the house at which point we'd be horizontal in the blink of an eye. He's the one and only person I've had sex with standing up in a doorway. Highly over rated and it wouldn't have been necessary if we could have had men in our rooms. I know now that the sex was fairly mediocre. So long as he was satisfied that was good enough. His mother used to mutter darkly about her husband being so rough he'd bruised her. I didn't stick around long enough to find out if their son would do likewise. He had a brother who looked nothing like him or his dad. I did wonder if the brutal sex his mother endured was payback.

In my final year at college men were allowed into our rooms but we had to leave the doors and curtains open. Not much joy there.

My route to independent consultant was not exactly orthodox. Half way through teachers' training college, I took a part-time job in a youth boxing club in Holland Park. My role at the youth club was to organise activities for the girls, who until I arrived came just to look at the boys. There's nothing wrong with that but they deserved more. Somehow I re-learned the rules of netball and got the girls to give it a go. I even ran around the court. This was a big challenge for me as I avoided exercise like the plague. At college I had very frequent periods to avoid going swimming.

The girls were all great characters and incredibly resilient. That experience generated a love of youth work that still lives on. For the first time the boys had to share their time on the football pitch with the girls. I also discovered that watching boxing matches when someone I knew was in the ring, was agonizing. To begin with I could hardly look but, by the time I left, I was shouting and cheering along with everyone else from the club. I can't remember there ever being a fight in the club, their aggression was channelled and disciplined. There were no drugs to worry about and they were too concerned about keeping fit to drink alcohol.

Having successfully completed my 3 years at college I took a teaching job immediately rather than do the extra year for a B.Ed. I also continued with the youth work. I frequently travelled home from Notting Hill Gate to Westbourne Grove and latterly to Kilburn and don't recall even once feeling anxious about my safety. Currently, in my nearby city I can't say the same.

Chapter 2

Out on my own, but not for long

In my first year out of college I shared a flat with a woman in Westbourne Grove. She worked for a famous author and was bisexual. I never met any of her friends, she was quite reclusive. The location was good as I was working in Aldgate and the tube station was close by. However the accommodation wasn't ideal because there were just 2 bedrooms and a kitchen. I had to go through her room to get to the kitchen. The only notable thing to occur there was we were burgled. Fortunately I'd got a big trunk where I kept my passport etc. I'd covered it with a rug and used it as a seat. They missed it but rummaged through my undies drawer. That was horrid and everything had to be washed. I couldn't afford to throw everything out and start again.

I didn't stay long after that and soon moved to a house in Kilburn. I hired a van to move my stuff and had to navigate Marble Arch and Hyde Park Corner for the first time, with no wing mirrors! I learnt that the best way to survive is to focus on where you want to go and go for it. Having survived Hyde Park and Marble Arch I moved into a house with two female singers and another woman. Because I was the last one in I got the damp room (flat roofed annex) at the end of the landing. With the exit from the flat of the non-singer I moved up to a room opposite the bathroom and next to the lounge, which housed the piano. I wasn't into opera in those days and the singing, which I'm sure was very good, did my head in.

In my last year at college I'd been seeing a tall gangly guy from Southampton. When he visited we were quite noisy and it upset them as much as their singing upset me. Anyway the killer was when a would-be model moved into the damp room. She virtually lived in the mould-ridden bathroom. No shower sadly. I moved out and split from my boyfriend around about the same time.

Having completed my induction year in a Girls' Catholic school in the East End of London, (I was so programmed), I moved out of teaching and into full time youth work. I might have stayed longer if I'd been allowed to teach just my main subject, biology. The Head figured that if I could teach biology I could also teach maths, erm no way, and religious education. I couldn't understand the logic and had to rehearse every maths and RE lesson the night before delivery.

Full time youth work was a strong lure despite having to work 10 nights a fortnight. I loved working with young people but my new boss was a weedy man and a creep who fancied himself as a psychologist. He set the centre up so that the young people had to come in the back entrance and navigate the activity hall to get to the reception area. The purpose of that was to identify those who were confident enough to walk across, rather than around the hall.

Back then we had to get the lads to hang up their Crombies by the front door in case they were carrying weapons. After a year in the LEA Youth Service I resigned and moved to the country. My rationale was that I would be Warden of a youth club, in charge! I learned later that the CEO who interviewed me, a lovely man, described me as a ball breaker. I have no idea what led him to that conclusion! Not long after leaving the London club, a young guy who did weight training there wrote and asked would I like to meet him. He was a couple of years younger than me and I had fancied the pants off him when I was working there but had been totally professional. I was sorely tempted but was already engaged. Who knows how things would have turned out if he'd written sooner?

The shock of leaving the bustle of London to work in a market town was a real challenge and I decided to get back to London within a year. Marriage, for all the wrong reasons, scuppered that. My ex was solid, responsible and ultimately boring. But he offered safety and security both of which had been lacking 'till then. My mother didn't like him, his mother didn't like me and I made a stupid decision.

Thinking back I married to avoid being in the same situation as my mother. For the first 6 months of my relationship with my ex we were totally sexually compatible. Then one evening, I looked at him and didn't want him to come anywhere near me. I avoided contact and just 'hoped I'd get over it'. Within a year we'd bought a house, got married and 'settled down'. Needing stability I foolishly thought the desire would come back. It didn't. Then followed 17 years of a secure and comfortable marriage largely bereft of sex. I would steel myself to have sex – for his birthday, for Christmas etc. but the frustration just grew and grew. I attempted suicide within the first year and took my only spell of sick leave, 2 weeks in 50+ years, to get over what was essentially a nervous breakdown. He kept a tight rein on me and even got to the point towards the end when, if someone asked me a question, he would answer for me. I kept taking the pill until I had to have a cone biopsy at which point I decided to be sterilized.

During this period my mother was diagnosed with lung cancer and died 4 months after she retired. She spent the last three weeks of her life in our house and it was heart breaking watching her decline. I have been a passionate anti-smoker since then. I've given up worrying about the smoke filled environment we grew up in. No point.

For much of the time I was married I worked in community education. I held two further roles as Head of Centre, the latter lasting 14 years with a promotion for the final four. The Centre I managed became a hub for a variety of age groups from mothers and toddlers to senior citizens. What I loved best were the youth club sessions. One of my first actions was to sack two bouncers who were paid to work at the discos. I found de-escalation to be so much more productive. It even worked when one very well-built lad had a police officer by the throat on the front doorstep. I just kept saying, 'Put him down,' and he did. I can't remember there being any repercussions except we had to ban the lad for a month.

Being part of watching them growing up was a privilege. Working with a great group of paid staff and volunteers we provided as rich a menu of experiences as possible and a safe place for hundreds of young people to be themselves. Our biggest challenges were the occasional fight and alcohol being smuggled in through the toilet windows. There are so many memories including trips to the seaside and ice skating, a disco boat trip to Holland and running across the park adjacent to the centre at 10pm with a member of staff, to stop a new boy from being beaten up. When we caught up with them they were so surprised they dispersed on sighting us. Just as well as I could hardly breathe. A call to the lad's school on Monday resolved the issue. Looking back I think we were so lucky not to have had any mishaps. Risk assessments weren't even a glimmer in anyone's eye.

On another occasion I had to ban one of the junior staff for punching another lad outside the club. When I asked why he had done it he said, 'I ran out of words.' That I could empathise totally did not mean I could let him off. In all of those years I only got one fat lip when I tried to break up a fight between two lads who were much bigger than me. My deputy at the time had retreated to the boy's loo and one of the voluntary staff stepped in and got one of the lads in a headlock. Between us we got them into separate rooms and got to the bottom of whatever the issue was. This was long before the days of safe handling/restraint were ever mooted.

I spent the coldest night of my life in a tent with a bunch of youth club members on an Army Youth Team night hike. Until around 11pm, when we were attempting to navigate through the forest, the soldiers sneaked up on us with thunder flashes. When we completed, unscathed and very wide awake, the chair of the management committee went off to sleep in his car. He next appeared fresh and warm when he emerged for breakfast. The rest of us slept fully clothed in a big heap in the middle of the tent. It took hours for us to be able to flex our limbs. The breakfast was the best I have had before or since. On another occasion we went to the base and took on the obstacle course climbing up and crawling under nets. Again no risk assessments done! But such fun!

For the final four years I took on the adult education brief, with around 40 tutors providing courses in the town and villages. That was a steep learning curve. I remember on my first day a woman came into my office and said, 'I'm your French tutor and I'm pregnant.' I hadn't a clue how to find another but fortunately she knew just the person. These were halcyon days before government strategy deemed that vocational courses would be funded and leisure classes such as keep fit, yoga and flower arranging would not. No matter that they could lead to a career and, at very least helped to keep people fit and sane.

Despite an interesting job and a good lifestyle that included two holidays a year, after nearly 17 years I couldn't stand it anymore. I had to sort the situation out for myself.

Chapter 3

Renounce perfection

My next step was promotion in 1988 to becoming an education officer – more responsibility and quite a lot more money. Freedom loomed and divorce was inevitable. My first CEO was probably the most impressive leader I have ever had the pleasure to work with. The epitome of an excellent leader, he had the amazing knack of being able to make everyone feel that they mattered and that he cared. In one of his speeches he spoke about energy creators and consumers. They are both so easy to spot – 'Yes we can' versus 'Yes but'. His deputy was another kettle of fish. On one occasion when he was briefing a group of us about restructuring, he finally said, 'You've had more of my time than you have a right to expect,' and stomped off. He'd been talking about our careers! Both the 'good cop and bad cop' moved on and I served under, not literally, two more CEOs.

Not long after taking up my post I met a very handsome Sri Lankan in Costa. Our eyes met and the atmosphere sizzled. Before long I took myself off to stay for a weekend with him. It felt like getting out of prison and the sex was amazing. He was hung like a horse. It was nothing more than a fling but, on returning home I began the tortuous process of separating and setting up alone. My husband was not happy but I settled for the bare minimum of cash and left most of the contents of the house behind. I should have bargained for much more because I'd earned more than him for the first 10 years or so, but I just wanted out.

I put a deposit on a brand new flat and not long afterwards my relationship with the love of my life (LOML) was in full swing. I met all of his family, we were as close as two people could be but I valued my hard gained freedom. We worked in the same organisation so saw each other every day. I still remember the first time we made love in his basement flat. It was right beside traffic lights at a busy city junction. I recall being very concerned about his health. He was lovely and we bonked like rabbits for five years. We had some wonderful holidays in assorted Greek islands, including Zante where the earth really did move, and we spent every weekend together.

My lovely Sri Lankan sent me cards from various parts of the world and then came to see me one Sunday. I was with LOML then, though not living together. They met and then we left LOML to go for a walk. That was it. I was totally hooked on LOML.

I was with him when his sister got married on a lovely summer's day, and I have some great photos of the two of us plus one of his uncle and me flirting. He was a very elegant man who reminded me of Tony Di Nozo's dad in

NCIS. Even on that occasion it never crossed my mind that we would get married. I'd been there. It never ever came up in conversation so I assumed the circumstances suited both of us.

'Learn to renounce perfection' has to be the daftest advice I have ever been given. That it came from the second CEO I worked with when I was an altruistic education officer made little sense at the time and even less looking back. I am after all a Virgo by birth date and by ascendant, a double dose of perfectionism. I remember bumping into her in the car park one evening around 7pm having been there since 7am. Her greeting was, 'Knocking off early?' She wasn't joking. Since then, with an MBA and years of delivering leadership and management training under my belt, I still haven't figured out what leadership style that was.

The best thing that the authority did for me was to sponsor me doing a Masters in Business Administration. Being in my forties I was the oldest one in the group of thirty. For three years I attended every Wednesday afternoon and evening and held down a full time job. That was the start of a totally different way of life. I learnt so much on HR, marketing, economics, statistics and much more. I became confident about speaking to and in groups. My blinkers were off! During this period I clocked up twenty-five years in the service of the authority. My reward was to be a rose bowl. Everyone who knew me knew that I was not a rose bowl type. I agreed with the leader of the council to accept it, be photographed shaking his hand, then go backstage and hand it back. The £25 would have been far more welcome.

In, 1994, '95 and '96 I used summer leave to volunteer in Bosnia. I've got reports, diaries and photos in abundance but there is little there that sits well with the content of this book. It was a desperately sad time and my feelings of helplessness and guilt, I could leave at any time, were very strong. Bosnia diaries need a book to do justice to the experiences. A key outcome from this was that LOML and I broke up. I was too consumed by work, studies and Bosnia and neglected him. He got married fairly soon after that to a woman who already had a daughter. I was devastated but had chosen my path.

The successor to 'renounce perfection' was little better. When I gave him advance notice that I was leaving to go freelance his response was, 'If you're a day late with your notice I'll make you work another month.' He could be quite inspirational but, at that moment, I knew deciding to launch myself as a freelance consultant, despite an enormous credit card bill, was less hazardous than staying put. He gate crashed my friends' only farewell do and told me, 'You know where we are when you need us.' I knew there and then I would put a red light outside my front door rather than go back. He gave me a huge bouquet of flowers, which I dropped off at the Children's Hospital en route home.

The decision hadn't been made lightly. Besides the legendary credit card bill I had the habit of spending my salary before I earned it, just like my mother. However the culture was dire, I was being bullied and it would not have been productive to make a case against the individual.

So I attended lots of training courses, in my own time, and finally decided I had enough contacts to make a start as an independent. For weeks before and after the move I would get up in the middle of the night to rework my finances. It was a gamble but it was necessary.

When I started my main sources of income were training aspiring headteachers, supporting schools on re-introducing performance management and working with governors and governing bodies on effective governance. Part of the training of aspiring heads took place in various parts of Germany, in British Forces schools. I did enjoy those trips and learnt a bit more about life in the army. One thing I remember being told was that, when wives need company when their partners are away, they put a box of OMO on the front windowsill – 'Old Man Out'. If only life were so simple!

Old **M**an **O**ut

I also made nine visits to Uganda to support the Government in delivering on its pledge to ensure

Universal Primary Education (UPE). There were highs and lows with this project. The key theme for me was that the pupils were desperately keen to get to school. Many walked in bare feet for miles only inches from busy roads with huge lorries thundering past. The contrast between them and some pupils in schools in England was very stark. A school might have a teacher, probably unpaid, sitting with a group of children under a tree. Their vision was very different to any of the schools back home, however impoverished they were.

Chapter 4

Internet dating and deal breakers

I got involved in Internet dating because I badly missed the LOML and I wanted to love and be loved like before. Work was hell, and the LOML, was still around until I went freelance. We had tearful lunches from time to time, remembering happier times.

My first venture into online dating was not inspiring – manic depressive in a woolly jumper. I saw him as I was looking for somewhere to park and almost carried on driving. Shameful to judge on appearances but sometimes... Life's short and spare time is precious.

I found it's a good idea in terms of security, to tell a friend where I was going, and the mobile number of the guy I was meeting. On a number of occasions I've popped to the loo to send a text saying – *'please call me asap. I need an out'*. Something similar happened with the guy in the hideous bright yellow shirt. I saw him long before he saw me but I did the decent thing and stayed long enough for a drink, which I paid for. By then I'd got more confident about taking my leave and I never committed in advance to a meal.

I learnt by experience. Choice of website - there are lots to choose from and I even tried an introductions agency at one point. I found that the agencies at the top of the search list were usually the best. Most sites asked for preferred age for a partner and then ignored it totally when they suggested 'matches'. This applied particularly when looking for a younger man, which was always my goal, (I'd had more than enough of older men in my youth), as too has been mind blowing, riotous sex. Mindful that some of my colleagues might also have been on the site I kept my messages quite chaste.

Then the user name. 'Lady Penelope' worked well for me. I got lots of messages, even marriage offers, from guys wanting to be my 'Parker'. The more important section is how you describe yourself. Words like tactile, passionate, sexy, sensual are all good but one has to be careful not to sound desperate. Lots of men do seem to be looking for someone to settle down with so I decided it was best to say something like, 'I'm not into 24/7, yet.' Despite that, a very long message, supposedly from an Italian, said, 'I want a wife who will do everything that she can to please her husband, one who will be a good wife.' He obviously hadn't read my bit of not 24/7 nor not joined at the hip. It sounded as though he was recruiting for a harem.

Then there is the section about height, weight, eye and hair colour etc. There's no point in describing yourself as slim if you're 5'4" tall, weighing 10 stone. They'll do the maths. Having said that, it is a challenge to decide whether one is average, athletic, slim, a few extra pounds or curvy. One can be slim and curvy surely?

I soon discovered I was wasting time and money by not posting a photo. So what if someone connected with work saw me? What were they doing on there anyway? Selfies especially with the camera in view look really naff so I relied on friends and events to get suitable shots.

Rightly or wrongly handsome young 'widowers', those earning £150k+, seeking 60-99 year old women, I viewed with deep suspicion. Those who couldn't spell were ignored. I'm drawn to fit, in the traditional sense, good-looking guys, with a higher level of education, cheeky, funny, and those who care what's happening to the planet, people and animals. Not necessarily in that order. Being good in bed and other locations is an absolute non negotiable.

As for weight, I became wary of the term 'large build'. On several occasions that has turned out to be belly popping out of shirt buttons, man boobs, would need two seats on an aeroplane, and totally oblivious to the fact they looked far from desirable.

When I got it together with a very charming colleague, during sex he kept telling me not to wriggle, to keep still!!! My 'wriggling' was a futile attempt to stimulate some sort of sensation, I realised an orgasm on my part was definitely not going to happen. Besides, I find it enjoyable to grind hips and other bits. I do like men who know when to take control, assuming they know enough about the female anatomy to make a success of that. He wasn't one of those.

In contrast a recent contact said he liked dominant women. He reminded me of a friend who was, maybe still is, on the game. She took it very seriously and made enough money to finance an extension to her house. She did a course to become a Dominatrix. I switched off at the point where she described nailing a man's testicles to the floor. She said she could easily get me work as a 'mature and sensual woman'. Bless her. I guess the lesson here is if your finances are a bit dodgy make sure you have a fall-back position. For a long time after going freelance mine was stacking shelves in the local supermarket. However a red light outside the door was also considered. Another friend, who lives across the road, volunteered to be the madam and to sit downstairs with a cricket bat.

She's a widow and we had some hilarious evenings with wine and DVDs. I'd often think I'd found a comedy only to discover it was nothing of the sort. We are both partial to Matthew McConaughey and there is one scene in Mud, when everything is still in the night and a shotgun blast rips through the walls. Both of us shot off our seats in shock and missed the next few minutes because we couldn't stop laughing. That's definitely more our scene than her downstairs with a cricket bat and me cavorting around upstairs.

I think I was in my mid 50's when I realised, that, for most of the men on sites, I was way past my sell by date. This has to be challenged! Why it is OK for men to expect to be paired up with females 20 even 30 years their junior, but it is questionable for a woman to want a younger man? One 73-year old man took it upon himself to lecture me, on the website, about my inappropriate behaviour. There's no logic here. Women generally take a lot more care of their appearance than men, throughout their lives. That has been the case with me.

Sex for the older woman is no big challenge. We don't have to get anything up and keep it up. Of course there may be a need for a little lubrication but there are assorted ways to deal with that. Having been on HRT for years it's not been something I worry about, but in any case plenty of foreplay including oral sex can overcome that little challenge. The other angle is that you may be approached by hopeful young men in their 20's who think having sex with someone old enough to be their granny is part of their rite of passage. Don't knock it till you've tried it!

I have been told that woman lie about their age and weight. I know for certain some men lie about their weight and their height. I remember meeting an academic in a Cafe Rouge. He was there when I got there and he remained seated throughout. We had a very animated conversation and when we stood up to go I thought in a moment of panic, 'Where are his legs?' He was as tall standing up as he had been sitting down and didn't even come up to my chin. I could have had him under the Trades Description Act!

Why is it that so many men want anal sex? A straw poll of my 4 nieces indicated that 75% of women go along with it. We were having dinner when one of my nieces said to another, 'I know how you do nooky.' The response was, 'so what' from two of her sisters. Fourth niece said, 'No way, ever!' The banter went on between the four of them for several minutes without being explicit. When I asked, 'Are we talking anal sex?' The look on their faces was priceless! Clearly the thought that their 68-year old auntie even knew about such things was beyond comprehension. I also knew how it felt to have medics rummaging around up there having had an operation for piles. I never want to go there again! Fortunately a cone biopsy didn't have the same effect on my psyche.

Another no-go area for me is licking my ears. Gross! Not only does it feel disgusting it also makes my hair all wet and then it goes curly! For some unknown reason one of my two cats, besides patting me on the face very gently, also tries to lick my ears. She's a rescue and thinks I'm her mother.

Politics and animal rights have always been hot issues for me. I remember meeting a guy in Marlow who had previously worked in South Africa. He turned up wearing a tatty pair of shorts, over spindly white legs, moccasins and a T-shirt that was buttoned up as far as he could go, (a size too small), with ghastly sweat marks in the arm pits. Over coffee he shared that he had had a perfectly healthy 3-year old German Shepherd put down in South Africa because he couldn't find anyone to take her when he returned to the UK. He thought quarantine would have been too distressing for her! My next question was, 'And where do you stand on fox hunting?' Another no brainer, he knew all the rules and regulations and clearly saw no harm in it. I knew the answer to my next question before I asked, yes he'd been a Tory his whole life. I guessed this because as soon as the Tories got back into power one of the first things they did was to try to repeal the ban on fox hunting. I remember writing a furious letter to the local MP. Something about only relevant to the green-wellie brigade poncing around on their horses in red jackets, swigging brandy and killing helpless animals. Interesting that, several years later, with COVID-19 still raging, the Tories boasted about horse racing starting up again.

He then proceeded to tell me a 'funny story' about how he'd got back together with his ex wife for the third time. He'd got 'bladdered' on the plane and then 'they were very naughty on the beach'. The thought of his white, spindly legs thrashing about in the sand did it. Enough! I went home. I've since added to my key questions, 'What's your take on global warming?' 'What's your stance on Brexit?' One lunchtime date explained away the climate crisis as, 'The world's been through many changes – the Ice Age, the Stone Age, it's a cycle and it will all revert.' His reason for wanting Brexit was, as a very small business owner, any goods he sold to the EU, customers had 100 days to return them, by which point they would be useless to him.

In another conversation on the Internet I asked, in all innocence, why was he attracted to older women. His answer, 'Because I don't have to worry about keeping up in bed,' struck a chill in my heart, and my nether regions. What did he think women of my age needed, wanted? For goodness sake!!

Another irritant is when men ask, 'what do you like'. Sometimes it's within the first few emails online, at other times it's when we've met for coffee. If there's chemistry they shouldn't have to ask. Things just progress. I'm certainly not going to say, 'Well we could start with a 69.'

I learnt to avoid those who 'are not very romantic'. That tended to means sex once a month is fine by them. Ironic or what? 'Tactile', or 'very romantic' are more promising. I learnt too that, 'an adventurous woman' is not one they can take mountain climbing. They usually expect their women to be bold and take the initiative in sex – positions and locations. Now I like the comfort of a sofa or bed or even draped over the banisters. (N.B. not for those who suffer from vertigo), in which case it's vital to hang on to the banister whatever. As mentioned previously, having sex in a dark alley is vastly over rated.

Chapter 5

Equality issues

Did you know that, once a woman turns 65, she can't even buy a cervical smear test! After having a cone biopsy I kept up with regular tests, paying for a test when the NHS stopped providing it free. Now, aged 71, I can't get one even though I'm prepared to pay. I followed this up with my MP pointing out that men with concerns about their prostate glands can get checked and treated until they die. The answer was that women over 65 are deemed to be so low a risk they don't need to be tested.

Surely that depends on how often they have sex and with how many partners! There seems to be an assumption that sex goes out of the window for women over 65. It's the same on dating sites. As I've already noted most men do not look after themselves as well as women do. Generally they seem to think they should not be seen dead with an older woman. I read a lovely news item about a 90+ woman whose husband died. When her doctor said to her, 'You must miss him,' she replied, 'I do, he had such a lovely penis.' She was a lucky woman, bless her.

The other issue I discovered over 30 years ago when still

married, is that a married woman can't be sterilized unless her husband consents! Had my ex refused I would have left him sooner than I did.

A simple rule of thumb is that women generally take much better care of their appearance because looking good makes them feel good. In my case, at the age of 71 whilst shielding from COVID-19, I'm so glad that I'm now blonde not brunette. My white roots are not immediately apparent after not seeing my hairdresser for 12+ weeks. As for the style I look increasingly like Boris Johnson on a very bad hair day. My legs, which haven't been waxed for the same amount of time, have driven me to revert to a razor. It only just coped.

With regard to sexual orientation I am straight. I have to admit to never fancying a woman. I know they can get strap-ons but I can't see how that would be an adequate substitute for a thick, long, throbbing penis, especially when Viagra is involved. That said my best friends are women.

In the past I was found attractive by two women, not at the same time thank goodness, and both were friends. The first never mentioned having a boyfriend and she never made a move on me. We were such good friends we went on holiday twice and nothing happened. I have never made any secret of how I lust after men and suddenly she stopped meeting me for dinner, cinema trips etc. It didn't occur to me that she might have been lusting after me until another friend, after a drunken night out threw herself into my bed.

We'd been out for a meal and booked a taxi so we could drink. When we were unloaded at the end of the evening we staggered upstairs chatting and laughing. She came into my room and pulled her top up to reveal the most perfect breasts. Unbeknownst to me she'd just had an operation because they'd drooped after childbirth. I was gob smacked and immediately asked where she got them done and how much it cost. It turned out she and her husband had done a lot of research, to cut that story short, I was on the case in no time. More of that later.

Returning to that night, having shown me her assets she leapt into my bed. I do have a spare bed but thought I won't be churlish if she wants to share mine. So I tentatively got in, as far away as possible. To my shock she leapt on top of me. I have to admit I was fascinated by her nipples. They'd obviously been removed and then stitched back on again. My observations were cut short when she rammed a finger or thumb into my vagina. Anything less erotic I have never experienced before or since. I must have pulled a face because, clearly disappointed, she looked down at me and said, 'Is that it?'

I was still speechless. With that she staggered into the loo and was violently sick. I noticed she had more tummy rolls than I had. I left her sound asleep the next morning when I went off to work. I hadn't slept a wink for fear she would throw up, choke and die in my bed. We never mentioned it ever again.

She did however introduce me to the Ann Summers rampant rabbit. Maybe she thought it might loosen me up. We were having lunch in Birmingham on a shopping trip and she asked the waiter where the nearest Ann Summers store was located. I was horrified! There was much sniggering when we paid up and left and headed to the shops. Now I had never been in such a shop before and I had no idea what many of the items were for. My friend soon enlightened me and I bought a rabbit. She'd bought one for her daughter because her husband kept falling asleep. Several weeks later my credit card bill arrived and there were items on it that I didn't recognize.

A call to the bank resulted in my having to go to the police station to get a case number. The rather masculine looking female officer asked which of the items on the statement weren't mine. It was tempting to say the Ann Summers item but I stuck to the truth. Suffice to say it was a really good bit of kit and I had loads of fun with it.

Now a cautionary tale. I had got chatting with a chap who said he was an inventor and had made a good living out of what sounded like very interesting work. We decided to meet up for lunch and he said he'd pick me up in his Jag. Just as we were ending our conversation he said, 'By the way, I have something to tell you.' He sounded vey solemn and so I replied, 'Go on then, you've only got one leg.' To which he replied, 'Yes.' To say I was mortified is an understatement. Nevertheless we met and he'd booked a table in a first floor restaurant. He was obviously a very gutsy man but sadly, there was no chemistry.

Chapter 6

Cosmetic surgery

So having viewed my friend's breasts up close, I was on a mission. Having been 34AAAAA I had always been desperate to have a bust. As soon as I could afford it I went for it. Top Harley Street guy, same one used by my friend, but not the best choice as it turned out. I did expand to 34C, but several years after the PIPs thing went viral, I got a letter saying he'd used PIPs. It had never occurred to me to check the paperwork because he was 'the best' and very plausible. I'd even seen him for a facelift in December 2006 and he didn't say a word about the scandal. In January 2012 he wrote informing me that I did have PIPs and should have a scan to see if they had ruptured. It was so long after it went public that I figured he was working alphabetically.

The results of that first facelift were very disappointing and he lied blatantly that he'd done under my eyes with no sign of stitches inside or out. I'd paid an extra £1k for that bit of the procedure. The upshot of the PIPs debacle was that both of mine had ruptured so I had them replaced and went for bigger. It's addictive. I sallied forth at 34DD very conscious that I had silicon floating around in my lymph nodes. Further down the line I learnt that a lifetime of maintenance is a side effect of implants.

As soon as I acquired breasts I splashed out on beautiful lacy underwear – matching bras, thongs, Brazilian briefs. I spent a small fortune, and wouldn't be seen dead in undies that didn't match. Going to the gym, I couldn't help noticing how many women had very unsexy undies. Washed out, different colours. Maybe it was just because they were going to the gym but…

Next up was another facelift with a new surgeon. I have always had heavy eyelids and was desperate to get rid of them. He did a good job on my chin and tidied up my ear lobes but my eyes, he was too cautious and I couldn't see much difference. To add insult to injury, when I came to, my throat and the roof of my mouth were red raw. Apparently I have a narrow trachea and his anaesthetist must have used an intubator that was too big. All other pain was nothing compared to that. The procedures do hurt but the feel good factor once the bruising goes is worth it. I found that high dosage Arnica was very helpful at speeding the reduction of bruising and there are products that help to reduce scar tissue.

Still not happy with my eyes I chose another surgeon. I wanted him to work on my eyes, face and tidy up my breasts, which had drooped. This one was a bit more gung ho and did make a tangible difference to my eyes. He also pulled up the skin on my neck by a bit more than an inch, so that all looked fine. He emphasised how difficult it had been not to damage the implants and boasted that very few surgeons could have done what he did. However, when I went for my next breast ultra sound, self-funded, I was told that both implants had ruptured underneath, precisely where surgeon three had cut and stitched to remove the 'banana effect'. When I went to see him he was clearly rattled and began by asking very gently, 'What did I want to do?' After very little discussion he then said, 'They need to come out and did I want to replace them.' That was a total no brainer. He added that in another 10 years I probably wouldn't be bothered. How little he knew!

A date was fixed and implants that were slightly more 'forward facing' were chosen. After the operation, which cost me £6k+, he was much more abrasive. When I went for my post op check he didn't shake my hand, invite me to sit down or look to see if everything had healed up properly. Instead he showed me a photo of what looked like two lumps of soggy jelly on a table. This was clearly intended to indicate that the implants were faulty and had, simultaneously, ruptured and leaked. I was genuinely upset by has manner and wrote to his PA to say so. By return there was a very apologetic response, he'd got a full client list that morning, it was his first day back after holiday... It might well have been his first day back but there was no one else in the waiting room when I went in to see him and no one waiting when I came out. However I gave him the benefit of the doubt and decided to ask him to do one more operation on my face, which I was still unhappy with. After a rambling monologue about a skin peel, a procedure which looked excruciating, he said he could do a small adjustment but didn't think it was a good idea.

To cap all of that, when I went for an ultra sound a couple of months later to check all was well, there was another hiccup. I was lying on the bed ready for the scan when in wandered a rather nervous looking woman in a white coat, not the doctor I usually see. She looked as though she had wandered in by mistake. Anyway she slapped oodles of gel onto the scanner/transducer and checked all over my right breast. 'All seemed to be alright.' Then she progressed to the left breast. She spent ages and I was getting quite worried, eventually she pressed so hard it hurt. At that point I said, 'I do have a pace maker in there?' 'Oh that's what those wires are!' Needless to say I wasn't billed and I got a second scan with my usual doctor that wasn't invoiced.

COVID-19 was the trigger to my final facelift. Prior to the official lockdown I had already decided to self-isolate after putting my car in for a makeover. I then was left with no income and no furlough pay as my accountant did an annual payroll for me. Initially I thought I'll just wait it out and eventually go back to visiting workplaces to conduct audits. Then I found I really liked not spending hours on motorways and getting up at 4.45am. A friend suggested the solution –

conduct business online. In a very steep learning curve I learnt how to host and join a zoom meeting. When I first saw my face on screen I was horrified. All I could see were wrinkles and baggy skin! My IT man advised me to stand my laptop on reams of paper so I looked up to it rather than down on it. It was better if I moved further away from the screen. Better still in dim lighting. Not good enough! I set about finding another surgeon to sort me out once and for all.

I finally settled on one and, in a zoom consultation, was totally honest about my encounters to date. I felt heard when he began by asking me, 'What were 3 things was I most dissatisfied with?' 'Just with my face?' I do have assorted other things I hanker after such as a tummy tuck.

After listening to my encounters to date and my motive for wanting further work done, he gave me the best ever list of options for my upper face, mid face and lower face. That was the first time anyone had approached it in that way. He gave me details of what could be done, together with pros and cons. His key message is that you get what you pay for. The next step, when the hospital reopens for private work, is to meet him face to face. I have already decided I want to leave my eyebrows where they are, I want fat transferred to my cheeks (on my face) potentially fulfilling two goals and I need to discuss options about sorting out my baggy chin.

Chapter 7

Holidays. Alone/with a girl friend/with a lover

After trying all three the best is definitely with someone you love and lust after. But I will come to that.

During my relationship with the LOML we had some wonderful holidays and were due to visit Israel. I can't remember why but a week or so before we were due to go he told me that he didn't want to go. It was too late to change anything so I decided to go alone. A big mistake. At the airport I was grilled by men in uniform about why I was travelling alone. In the resort I was regarded as fair game every time I went for a meal or a walk. The women, by and large, were just plain hostile. I did visit Mt Sinai, the Dead Sea and Jerusalem but I was not comfortable, came home early and LOML was very pleased to see me back.

Apart from my ex the only man I've been on holiday with was LOML. One of the funny things that struck me was that whereas my ex would do all the tripping around for drinks, snacks etc. it was quite a shock, to find that LOML expected us to take turns. Funnily enough it felt quite liberating. Everywhere we went, be it the Lake District or sunspot, we had blissful times. In Portugal we played squash as well as sightseeing. In every location we quickly became acquainted with the local wines and stray cats. On our first visit we found a litter of very small kittens in undergrowth just up the road from our apartment. We fed them cat food every day and left a message in the apartment for those coming after us, asking would they look out for them.

It's been 26 years since we parted and I haven't quite given up hope of finding someone else who I could share my life with, but not 24/7, and I'm not holding my breath.

Whilst I have had some great holidays with longstanding women friends, mainly to Italy, I will never ever go on holiday with a woman again unless we have separate rooms. I really need space to retreat to. This was especially so on a trip to New York just before Christmas one year. To be fair I was completely knackered, (because of work!), and it was freezing, freezing cold in NY. My feet were like blocks of ice throughout.

The first sign of trouble was when my travelling companion wasn't interested in visiting Macy's or Bloomingdales. She was only interested in following in her parents' footsteps when they'd travelled from Hungary years previously. She'd omitted that fact in the planning of the trip. Had I known I would have been prepared for separate programmes.

The second was when we went out for our first dinner. She suggested we share the main course because the servings were quite large. Now I have a very healthy appetite, especially when it comes to chips, and I don't share my dinner with anyone unless it's a dish meant for two. This is a woman whose house sat on land worth at least £1m per acre. She and her husband both had good pensions and she was doing well out of part-time tutoring.

The next day my concerns were compounded when we went into an obviously cheap diner. I immediately spotted chilli and rice and that was me sorted. I ordered it. She on the other hand asked how much would it cost? I walked away as far as I could. Suffice to say I blew £3k, I can't remember what that was in dollars, on a pair of diamond earrings, which were exactly what I'd been looking for, and she spent $3 on a plastic dinosaur for her grandson. That's why she's rich.

The worst bit was her sycophantic approach to people like guards on the metro. She'd look up at them fluttering her eyelashes and rabbit on about how brilliant they were, how helpful, how lovely blah, blah blah. She'd done the same with me and it had grated, this time it really rattled me. From her perspective she thought I was really difficult to live with when stressed. Definitely not a win-win situation.

The situation wasn't helped because we were in a hotel with no bar! Can you imagine that? To get out of the room we shared I'd retreat to the bar next door or the swimming pool on the top floor of the hotel.

Anyway, just when I thought I was going to escape, Heathrow closed because of snow and we were stuck. I freaked out and disappeared to the computers in the lobby to see if I could find us another way home. Her first thought was 'extra cost'. I remember squeezing out through clenched teeth, 'I'll pay.'

Having spent hours on the net I found us a way home via Chicago. Meanwhile she had gone for a walk and I needed her passport number to make the booking. She finally ambled in several hours later by which time there were no seats left. Now she'd had a shoulder operation before our trip so I suggested we play on that plus the fact that I have high blood pressure, a pacemaker and I'm supposed to avoid stress. It worked and we got out.

Not having learnt my lesson I agreed to a touring holiday in Peru, with another girlfriend. We'd paid for 4/5 star accommodation and what we got was very basic. We went in August, which was, of course, winter in Peru. Waiting to be picked up from the airport I almost froze.

I'd never done a tour before and found that being with the same people almost 24/7 tiresome. There would be toilet stops, we'd stay at some locations long after I'd seen what I wanted to see. The condors drifting overhead on the thermals were awesome but 20 minutes is plenty. Besides I have red kites flying overhead at home that do the same thing. I agree the scenery isn't quite so spectacular but... At one point we stopped for a loo break and everyone dutifully got off. Although I was bursting I sat there thinking I will not be told when to pee.

The accommodation was disappointing. In one place it was basically a cupboard that the two of us shared. In another it was like I imagine youth hostels to be. Now I do like to give vent to my feelings and so I grumbled quite a bit. Once I've vented I get on with it, whatever 'it' is. My companion on the other hand would put up with anything. 'Oh it's not too bad', was her favourite phrase even when the freezing wind whistled off Lake Titicaca and through the huge gap under a window. We slept in our clothes and still froze.

By the time we got to Cusco, which was really interesting. I'd had enough of being cold, living out of a case and the lack of autonomy. I refused to trek up to Machu Picchu and moved into a luxury hotel in the town. I spent hours in the Internet café communicating with the friends I missed, I bought a fabulous pair of onyx earrings and I felt human again. When the group got back my friend was laid up with a tummy bug so she was fairly quiet. Then the day came and off we went to airport only to find there had been a bird strike and our plane was to be filled with people who had not been able to fly the previous day. A total blow made worse by the announcement that they would find us a hotel for the night. Next day we turned up again and got on the plane and there we sat for what seemed like eternity. The delay was because the hold was overloaded. No need to panic. When we eventually got airborne the worry became would we miss our connecting flight in Germany. We did. Yet another night in a hotel. I sobbed my heart out which I think shocked my friend.

Chapter 8

The long termers and heart breakers

There are three men who were part of my life for around 20 years. The first, a smouldering, leather jacketed, Italian. He is a lecturer and seems totally unaware of his appeal. We met on the Saturday and he didn't go home till Monday. Such fun and really challenging intellectually. His focus was on maths and sociology. He literally oozed sex appeal. Our sexual encounters were marathons, each of us wanting more. We both loved oral sex and, apart from deep penetration, the 69 position is my favourite. I do find it hard to be unselfish at a certain point and my other worry is that I'll do serious damage just after that point. Sometimes we'd do it with me on top, which was a departure from the norm. Any inhibitions I had, I lost, and it was such fun.

Alas he got headhunted to the States and our encounters reduced to once or twice a year. Our most recent encounter I thought might be the last. He spoke about buying a house and settling down. Every moment I spent with him, he made me feel that I was the most desirable creature on the planet. That is a gift. Our farewells, when I dropped him at the station were film worthy. We've been in touch again recently over the demonstrations about George Floyd. He said it all felt surreal. He also said that he was hoping to come over soon and would be looking me up. Watch this space.

Then there is a drop dead gorgeous Adonis. A lawyer and everything for him was very clear-cut. Not a woolly thought in his head. We'd arranged to meet in the restaurant of a hotel at a motorway junction. I was sitting down when he arrived and I just looked up and up... He looked like a film star and again appeared to be totally unaware of his impact on me and doubtless many other women. We had dinner and he dropped me back at my car. I really didn't expect to see him again. However on the second occasion we had dinner and then I gave him a blowjob in a side street off Baker Street – it just felt right at the time. It's etched in both our memories and he does remind me from time to time. It was quite challenging driving to his flat in West London with both of us in a state of high arousal.

On another occasion I remember us having dinner locally and the waiter who I knew quite well, asked, 'Where are you off to next?' My response was, 'Home for riotous sex.' The waiter had had sex with my friend on her kitchen table so I knew he could stand the teasing but my date's face was a picture! He always gave me brilliant oral sex and is totally unselfish. Unfortunately he does have erectile dysfunction. I remember the first time we attempted sex his penis was flaccid. He kept saying to me, 'You're not letting me in.' I was desperate to let him in and we did manage it from time to time but he was better with oral sex. Our encounters now are limited to when his wife is out of town. The last time I saw him, I didn't take my clothes off because I had got involved with a very lusty builder. We still chat from time to time.

The third was a military man and I'll describe that relationship later.

Every now and again a 'someone special' has just popped up in my life. This was true when I put my flat on the market. The first person to view was waiting for me when I got back from work. He walked towards me with a beaming smile and then spoke in a Scottish accent. I do so love a Scottish accent. Anyway I showed him around and he asked if he could come back for another look. I replied, 'Of course, if you bring a bottle of wine.' The next time he came round we sat on the sofa and got closer and closer. Finally he asked, 'Can I take you to bed?' 'I thought you'd never ask.' Sex with him was fun, relaxed and immensely satisfying.

Very soon in our relationship he told me about a girl he'd had a relationship with when he'd visited Australia. She became pregnant and had an abortion, only telling him after it was done. He showed me some of the emails they'd exchanged and she was clearly very angry with him. He was adamant that he wouldn't go back to her but he did want to emigrate to Australia. By this time I was in too deep. He was practically living at mine and helped me move into the house I bought 2 miles down the road. He bought my flat. Foolishly I thought he wouldn't go. Anyway, to cut a long story short, he went. Yet again, I was devastated.

About a year later he phoned one Sunday morning and said he was missing me. He told me he'd been seeing a Hawaiian woman but it was me he wanted. We spoke every week, he gave me websites of houses in Australia to look at, and eventually met when he came back to the UK for a holiday. Despite the big build up things didn't feel right. We made love, drank champagne but I knew something had happened. Eventually he admitted that the woman was gutted when he finished with her, and had turned up in Australia and was staying in his house. They'd reconciled.

I rationalised it by reminding myself that I had no desire to live in Australia but it took me a while to get over him.

In due course I went back to the dating site. Fairly soon I got chatting to an extremely good-looking guy who lived in St Albans. We made contact just before Christmas, and, after a few days we arranged that he would come to my house and we'd go out from there. That's not usually a good idea but I did alert my friend across the road. He was tall, blond, muscular – but not overly so. We went for a walk, had dinner and went to bed. It was lust at first sight. The next three days were amazing. The best sex I'd ever had. I became much more 'adventurous' and was completely knackered every night. Bliss.

I learnt that he was in IT and was working in Holland Monday to Friday and back home Friday night-Sunday night. So every Friday he would arrive around 8.30pm and stay till 6-7pm on Sunday. Initially that suited me fine because I was establishing my business and working stupid hours. I took him to meet my friends and they liked him. When we were out together women were always eyeing him up. The first alarm bell was when he told me how he'd gone to Italy to meet the parents of the girl he was seeing before he met me. Whilst there he told her he was finishing with her. However by then I was completely hooked.

Before I met him I'd had a number of fainting spells and, after 7 years of fainting in a variety of shops, my then doctor suggested she could refer me to a neurologist. I jumped at the offer, said I would pay, and was seen within a few days. The consultant was convinced I was fainting not fitting which I knew already, and initially told me to take life easier. Mission impossible! Anyway the tipping point was when I fainted at the wheel of my car whilst en route to pick up my brand new car. (I have a thing about sporty cars). The experience was horrendous. I was stuck in a queue of traffic and couldn't get off the road. As with each syncope (fainting spell), except the first, I felt it coming on. On this occasion it felt like my head was being wrenched over my left shoulder. I woke up 20 minutes later in an ambulance being given oxygen. The police drove my car to the hospital and told me they were reporting me to the DVLA and I was not to drive until my condition was sorted.

That night, my guy, arrived from Holland and couldn't have been more understanding. A few days later I went back to see the neurologist who referred me to a cardiologist. After several more days I got to see the cardiologist who did a simple test-compressing my carotid artery. I was lying down at the time. Basically I flat lined and he diagnosed a condition called Vaso-Vagal Syndrome. It can start at any age and usually gets worse with age and stress. We discussed options and the only viable one was to have a pacemaker inserted. I asked when it could be done, he replied 'tomorrow'. That was just before Easter and I was due to visit what felt like 'my partner' in Amsterdam so we agreed I would go in the following week.

The weekend was a bit strange. It was very cold, even the posh hotel was freezing, but we got out and about. I was terrified that I'd faint again and anxious about the operation. The cardiologist said there was a 90% success rate. Obviously I'd have preferred to know I was spending £8k on a guaranteed solution. Any way I had the operation on Thursday and took a taxi to work in London on Monday morning. I did several more days like that and was shattered by the end of the week. The second alarm bell was when my partner said he was signed off sick for two weeks. There was some suggestion that the clients didn't like his management style. I didn't think too much about it and he settled in with me and drove me to my various bookings during his two weeks sick leave.

The first big blow up was when, still within 6 weeks of the operation, I started using public transport. My train was delayed and it took me hours to get home. He'd bought fish and chips and put them in the oven. By the time I got to the station, 2 hours later, he was incandescent. In the 4 miles to home he reduced me to a sobbing heap. Basically he harangued me about how useless I was. He had a particular approach which he later told me was called 'change control'. This meant that he'd argue a point and then suddenly introduce a new topic of conversation. It was very disconcerting.

He eventually calmed down and he we had a quiet weekend. Six weeks after the operation, and thanks to the amazing support of my surgeon, I was given my licence back. I was ecstatic. My partner was there when I got the phone call and he didn't even smile. He appeared completely disinterested.

Having had the all clear at the hospital I returned to the gym. The following day my left arm had ballooned and he rushed me to A and E. The medics thought I had a clot in my arm but nothing showed up on the ultrasound. One of the nurses said, 'Don't worry you're not going to die!'

My partner was brilliant, very supportive. The upshot of all of that was that I had to have heparin injections in my stomach every day for a week and I also had to take warfarin tablets. My friend across the road has two daughters one of whom is a nurse. Whatever time I got home I would go across the road and she would give me the injection. For that I am eternally grateful. The implications of the warfarin meant that I had to have daily blood tests to get the right dosage. I was a complete wreck, juggling working and driving madly in breaks to the health centre for blood tests.

One Friday I phoned the hospital to ask about my blood tests. Were they normal? The response was, 'Oh they're nowhere near normal!' That evening I phoned my guy to ask what time he'd be over. He replied, 'I'm not coming, I don't want to watch you die.' That was 12 years ago.

I pleaded with him and weeks later he came over, we had

sex and then he told me he had to get back because he was seeing a nurse. Nevertheless I asked him to keep my door key. When he got home he texted to say he'd put it in a vase on my windowsill. Several weeks after that he offered to come over then cancelled on the day saying that things had changed between him and his female neighbour, over the weekend, and they were now a couple. He had often mentioned her, how she'd pop round for a drink.

What I learnt from all of that is what doesn't kill you definitely makes you stronger. I read a really useful book called 'Manage your mind' and made a list of 10 things not to do in future. The only trouble was that, as with rescue remedy, which I keep in my bag at all times, when I needed it most I forgot I had it.

Next up was the epitome of the wolf in sheep's clothing. He's still in and out of my life and I care about him more than is wise. Longish, wild grey/blonde hair, eyes you could drown in, approached me on the website. I put him off because he was too far away. He persisted and finally came to my house to plug some holes, in my ceilings(!!), taking two days in the process and staying two nights.

The first night he stayed the atmosphere was quite charged. On the second evening after dinner, he looked at me and said, 'Cuddle?' In less than a minute his tongue gave me the first of many orgasms. He was a builder, fabulous body, didn't bother with underwear, a walking sex machine. Every time I unzipped him and freed his throbbing penis I was lost in the moment. There was a seriously big vein running up his penis, the merest whisper of a touch and BOINGGGG, he was ready for action. At 57, 11 years younger than me, the oldest man I have ever had sex with. He could keep going for hours. My stamina increased exponentially, I was completely smitten. He sent me my first ever 'dick pic'. I wasn't wearing my glasses when I looked at the picture and thought, 'Why is he giving me the finger?' Never mind that he was a twice-divorced bankrupt. Bring it on!!! He really got to me but it didn't last, and only gradually have I reached a stage where I'm happy with just the regular texting and occasional encounters.

Chapter 9

Military men and other noteworthy encounters

To be fair I've only interacted with three military men and two left much to be desired.

I met my dusky and hunky SAS Captain via a newspaper. We first met in the Officers' Mess at the local RAF base. He was there for refresher parachute training, and in full camouflage gear. My first thought was OMG! We went for dinner and the atmosphere was intense.

He beamed in and out of my life pretty consistently, a bit like the chocolate box man, usually between missions/projects. Often I've been around home when he's called but there was one time when I was the one out of the country. I was working in Jinja, Uganda and, when he phoned, was standing knee deep in a bath in a hotel on the edge of Lake Victoria. On the top of the water was a layer of dead mosquitoes and other assorted insects. My insect exterminator was working overtime. Outside the frogs were in full throat and it was quite difficult to hear him. He seemed quite surprised to hear where I was. More usually I'd visit him at the base or he'd come to the flat. Visits to the base always began with the same question at the gate, 'Is your visit personal or for business?' Even at 8pm on a Saturday night, when he'd just returned from some far-flung hot spot. The guards were very discrete, never a smirk in my presence. There was something quite romantic about lying in his bed listening to planes arriving and taking off. Sadly he wasn't blessed with an effective penis yet anyone he didn't respect he would label 'a limp dick'. I never had the heart to comment. I liked the sense of intrigue, living vicariously.

I remember once when visiting me he parked his jeep in someone else's parking space. This was of course challenged by the aggrieved neighbour. I've never seen anyone back off as quickly as he did when my visitor appeared beside me in the doorway. It was quite fun while it lasted but I think that was because I love reading spy stories, crime thrillers etc. I liked the 'mystique', and loved hearing his views on world events.

The Cotswold hunter was another, more recent, encounter on the Internet. His photograph showed this guy on a horse, with cowboy hat and gun. I enquired on the site why he was dressed like that. It transpired that local landowners paid him to shoot foxes. When I pursued my questioning around galloping around killing helpless animals, his responses quickly generated into – stupid woman, you don't understand. You're clearly not listening to me.

I'm sure there are women who will think he cuts a dashing figure, I regard him as a thoroughly unpleasant man, to be avoided at all cost.

My biggest regret is not inviting a gorgeous Spaniard to my bed. I met him on my third trip volunteering in Bosnia in 1996. He was on a monitoring mission with UNPROFOR, the UN Protection Force. I was researching material for a resource pack for secondary school students. When I stepped into his makeshift office he uncurled himself, walked towards me and smiled. I was *sooo* smitten. During the conversation we discovered that we were both going to be in Split on the same night, he for work, and me to travel home. We arranged to meet for dinner in the Hotel i. During dinner he offered to take me to the airport the next morning. At the end of dinner he asked could he join me in my room. He said, 'You will not regret it.' I was torn. He'd told me he had a wife and children back home and I was anxious about not sullying the reputation of the aid agency I was volunteering with. I said no. What planet was I on?

He phoned when I got to my room and said he still wanted to take me to the airport, which he did. Holding my hand, we said our goodbyes. He sent me a card afterwards, but with no return address. I have kept his photo and the card and I did have a go at searching the net without success. I so wish I had not been so 'decent'. As a result of writing this I dug out some cards and messages, mainly from people thanking me for assorted support. In the midst of those I found 3 cards dated 1996 and 1997, from my lovely Spaniard, and his work address. On one message he had written, 'he'd tried to call me but couldn't connect' and at the bottom, 'please don't answer'. On the other two he asked me to let him know about my life. I don't recall noting that at the time I received them, so 24, years later, I have written to the address he gave me and asked if they could forward my letter. Seize the moment. Life is short.

My next serious encounter was with a very, very intense man, a war photographer, who came by train from Warwick (I quickly discovered from the alcoholic rehab). Totally lovely, sexy, adorable when sober, but could down a bottle of vodka in one go. He didn't even swallow. From which point he'd lie, steal, cheat, do anything to get more.

We dated for about five months during which time he fell off the wagon twice. At one point he was more or less living at my flat. I loved seeing his photos and hearing his stories about Afghanistan. He gave me an Afghani bank note, which I have kept to this day.

His grandmother lived in Rugby and she stood by him through thick and thin. I drove him there once when he became too much to handle. Subsequently I visited him there and we made love in the spare room whilst his grandma watched TV in the next room. Very sweet, and very intense. I also visited him when he was back in the Warwick rehab. I was so keen for intimacy that he was the one saying, 'Sshh, wait.'

He came back to me sober but soon became quite manic. Eventually I had to have the police remove him. I put all his stuff in bin bags and left them in the hall for him to collect. That was a hard lesson about not thinking love can change everything.

One of my most romantic encounters was on a train. I first became aware that a rather handsome, bald man was staring at me, when I saw his reflection in the window. He had asked if I had finished with the paper but then didn't read it when I handed it over, just stared at me. When I arrived at my stop he got off too, glued to my shoulder. Apparently he'd spotted me in the morning and couldn't believe his luck when I was there again in the evening. These things happen! We had a coffee during which time he told me that his partner was arriving imminently from Liverpool to live with him. Like the good woman I am (hmmm) I said, 'I don't do married men.' We then went off regretfully in opposite directions. I looked for him every time I got the train to London. Several months later, returning from a conference, I found myself face to face with him exiting the train home. Crash, bang, wallop! We made it to the station exit whereupon he swept me off my feet and kissed me, very passionately. I didn't resist. Why would I? He walked me to my car where we had a brief explo, (thank heavens for my lovely, sexy undies), and three days later he visited me at home. We didn't even get beyond the sofa and I'm sure you can guess the rest.

He came to my house regularly until his partner got a mega lucrative job in Liverpool and off he went. I thought that was quite inconsiderate of her.

There have been a number of others but I think I'll leave it here.

Chapter 10
Cats and other friends

With some very notable exceptions I prefer animals to people. That said I love my friends as much as I love my cats. When we meet each of them usually talks about their grown up children, their job and then they say, 'How are your cats?'

Cats have been a huge part of my adult life. I have lots of cards and books about cat behaviour. My favourite is one that says, 'Behind every gifted woman there's often a very talented cat.' The two who choose to live with me at the moment are both rescues. I shall call them Boggins and Scramble to protect their identity. Boggins came first. I adopted her when both my elderly cats had to be put to sleep because of kidney problems. I couldn't stop crying and the vet phoned me to ask would I take an abandoned kitten. They said she had a broken pelvis, although they hadn't X-rayed her. I went to see her and it was love at first sight, on my part.

I was told I had to keep her in a cage so that she didn't further damage her hip. So I got her all set up in a big cage in my study with water, food, litter tray and comfy bed. She howled so much that I let her out after a very short time and gave her the run of the study thinking she couldn't come to much harm. In minutes she was exploring the surface of my desk! Her other trick was to lie against the door with her paws poking through to the landing, howling piteously. I opened the door one morning and she shot down the stairs.

Seriously worried by this point I took her to the animal hospital in Swindon where a very charming German vet checked her out. As he gently tapped her knee to check nerves, she bit right through my thumbnail. Bless her. Well his verdict was that she did have a broken pelvis and it was too late to risk re-setting it. I asked what I should do with her painkillers. 'You take them.'

We returned home and I soon realised that she must have been badly mistreated. She was particularly anxious about feet. If I got too close she would sink her claws in and or bite. Unfortunately she did the same with visitors particularly those who dangled their feet whilst having a meal. Many is the time I threatened to take her back, but that's now twelve years ago.

I have numerous pieces of trellis on my garden walls and on the outside of my gate. She climbs up those like spider man to go for very short wanders around the outside of the house. Unfortunately there was a thug of a cat next door, another rescue, who reckoned he was lord of all he surveyed. He chased her as she was trying to climb the gate and bit her tail. That turned septic and it took three of us at the vet to try to get antibiotics into her. At one point this tiny cat was lying on her back hissing, spitting, claws extended. All three of us stepped back and I said, 'You have to admit that's impressive.' The vet resorted to a crush cage. Once in the cage she tentatively jabbed the syringe into Boggins' rear end at which point she leapt straight up in the air and hissed and spat alarmingly. The vet jumped back, leaving the needle in Boggins' bum. I don't know which of the four of us was the most traumatized. Boggins did get her own back. Thug was sleeping against the outside of my garden wall and she leapt down on him and took a chunk out of his head. Justice, but it didn't ease relationships. He has since died and Boggins has taken on his role. She has the unnerving habit of running into the road when a car comes into the close. Instead of running across to the other side she sits in the middle of the road. I have no idea how many lives she has used up. There have been two new cats in the close and she has made it very clear who is top cat.

I didn't risk taking her back to the vet who I knew was afraid of her and switched to a new vet in town, by chance an Italian male. Be still my beating heart! Anyway I gave him fair warning and took her along to be seen for the first time in years. It all passed in a bit of a blur. He didn't risk cutting her claws and when I asked if her teeth were ok he replied, 'Oh I've seen them and they are just fine.' Now at least I can get worm tablets and flea treatment without pretending they're for

Scramble. Maybe she'll have mellowed a bit more before we go back in a year's time.

Six months after rescuing Boggins I adopted Scramble from the local cat sanctuary. To be more accurate he adopted me. He came towards me with his tail up straight, purred and rubbed himself against my legs. I brought him home after he'd been checked out and Boggins went ballistic. It was her house, I was her mother, who was this interloper? It was hell for ages. Even now after almost eleven years he gives her a wide berth. They fight about who gets to sleep on my bed which can be very disconcerting when woken from a deep sleep. When I have a man in my bed I have to shut the cats out of the bedroom. This unites them and they spend most of the night scratching the door and standing guard. If, in the heat of the moment, I forget to shut the door Boggins likes to get up close and personal. On those occasions I look around to see two pairs of eyes watching me. She's very loyal and just likes to make sure that the moans and groans don't mean that I'm being dismembered.

One morning I was awoken to the sound of Scramble growling. As I came to I asked what the matter was. I was jolted awake as the thug from next door walked past my bedroom! I screeched and leapt out of bed wearing only perfume. By the time I got downstairs thug had got Scramble backed against the sofa. I had to save my cat! I threw the patio door open and shouted as loudly as I could 'Get out, get out and don't come back. I followed him into the garden and he sauntered slowly and arrogantly along the wall. Then I realised I was stark naked and thought about the neighbours. None of them ever mentioned it although I did get some funny looks. Since then I have kept a broom in the garden and, on numerous occasions I have charged down the garden wielding it like some giant spear.

One of the benefits of lockdown is that I'm home all the time. Boggins, as ever is my shadow, but she's not nearly so resentful when it's Scramble's time for a cuddle.

I've introduced two friends to Internet dating and one found her one true love on her third date. She is still a very good friend and I love him to bits too. We have lunch from time to time as threesome and it's very comfortable. She and I had a great evening for my 71st. We went to see Magic Mike. Such fun! Sadly all we got was the glimpse of one bum. Maybe the late evening show is more revealing. Anyway several of my friends want to go so that's an idea for my 75th. The female compere was a total laugh. She had us all up singing and waving our arms around. We had our photos taken with 3 of the guys at the end of the show. The dancers were brilliant. The drinks were exorbitant.

Another 'friend' was all over me like a rash when she moved up from the south coast and didn't know many people. I foolishly let her monopolise every Friday night, and we did have fun. Then along came, 'Michelin Man', a barrel chested, arrogant little man. In no time at all they were glued to each other's sides. I gather he was into Tantric sex. It got to the stage that she and I would arrange to go out for a meal and, like clockwork, he would strut in at 9pm, even though they were living together. I tried the subtle approach of taking my leave 10 minutes after he arrived. That didn't work so eventually I asked why she could no longer handle a whole evening with me without him tagging along. Just because she loved him didn't mean I would even like him. That was pretty much the end of our friendship.

After that she would contact me once a month to ask if I fancied dinner but I'd lost my appetite.

I have been immensely fortunate to have some amazing women friends. They are a mix of women, doing challenging jobs, and others who focused on family rather than career. At different times we have been there for each other. I survived a second and third suicide attempt, mainly because I don't cope well with rejection so you can probably figure out when they happened. I was very serious each time. I didn't want to be there in the morning. I'd made provision for my cats in my will, I didn't care about anything else. After the third attempt I was made to see a counsellor. I realised then that I could be sectioned which would remove any power I had over my life. So I convinced him I wouldn't try again. In his report he described me as, 'highly assertive and highly needy'. What a rubbish combination. Pretty much continuously since then I have been on anti-depressants. The weight gain from those and HRT are a small price to pay for equilibrium. Most of them knew nothing about these events but it was my friends I turned to afterwards. We sparked off each other, encouraging and inspiring each other not just to survive but to enjoy and often laugh at life and work. I love them to bits.

Chapter 11

Keeping fit for purpose

Whilst sex is great exercise, if I don't have it regularly it's not enough to keep me truly fit.

I heard that swimming is the best all round exercise you can get, and non-weight bearing. Failsafe you might think. So it was until some hulk surfaced underneath me and broke two ribs. I'm not a strong swimmer and I don't cope well with waves. When I recovered I sought out quieter times for over 60s. Even then there were, mainly men, hammering up and down creating their own tsunamis, so I gave that up. I need my own pool.

As for squash, fabulous exercise and great if you have anger issues. I started playing in my 40s with the LOML. There is no more satisfying feeling than when the ball connects with the racquet in a shot that can't be returned. That lasted until some diehard male decided he could reach the unreachable and sent me hurtling out of his way and into the wall. There I sat checking fingers, wrists etc. and working out if I could still do my freelance work. (No sick pay). Some people I know just book a court for themselves and have a good thrash about. I tried that in my late 60s and for some reason my feet felt they were glued to the floor but my body kept going. Result I crashed into the wall and sat there wondering if I'd got concussion. I'm convinced there was something wrong with the soles of my trainers.

At some point someone suggested the gym and I learnt quickly 'the gym' tends to offer two options –fitness classes and do it yourself on assorted equipment designed to exercise and build muscles. Cardio, running and rowing get your blood racing, and power weights build or maintain muscle tone. That's the sum total of my understanding. I booked an induction session and launched forth.

I quickly discovered that fitness classes were not an option even though they look like great fun and there are always queues of people lining up, ready for action. I like music and often have a little dance around my kitchen whilst the radio blares out music from the 60s, 70s and 80s. However as soon as I join a fitness class I forget which is left and which is right and end up going the opposite way to everyone else. Either that or I'm around 20 seconds behind everyone else. Probably a bit irritating for most others in the class and there's no point in ignoring the obvious. So I am left with the solo option.

My first gym was a joy. It was owned by a young couple, very close to home and with a lovely pool. Sadly they were taken over by a chain and the ethos changed. The gym trainers/minders were more interested in doing their own exercise than in helping others. The tipping point was when, in full view of a member of staff I tried to lift off two 20kgs weights, not at the same time, to swop them for two 10kgs weights. I succeeded, watched by the member of staff. He grinned and said, 'It was fun watching you do that.' I replied, 'I am completely underwhelmed by your support.' His reply, 'You should have asked.' Suffice to say I went looking for a new gym.

The second has changed hands several times. The contract is managed by the District Council. It caters well for people of all ages with and without disabilities and it runs cardio rehabilitation sessions. Pre-COVID-19 I got chatting to a man at one of those sessions. We were side by side on the recumbent bikes. I was gasping for breath at level 3 and he was pushing level 9. Turned out he was 78 and, prior to his operation refereed national level basketball. He'd had a quadruple bypass and his surgeon had promised to get him fit for the new season. Awesome!

The gym is a great place for people watching, but not so good if you're looking to make friends. Most people are there to do what they've got to do then get on with everything else. Whatever doubts I had about my size or fitness level, I forgot them! I was competing against myself. It became addictive. I didn't have fixed days to work out but usually went mid afternoon. That got me home in perfect time for a glass of wine. No matter what afternoon I went, there were a few men and women who were always there! Those women don't have an ounce of fat on their bodies and some of the men have brilliant bodies-broad shoulders, slim waists and solid muscle from shoulders to toes. A joy to behold and where else would you get to see them for a trivial monthly fee? Not nearly as titillating as watching rugby but still... I was so enthralled by one guy's physique I told him he should carry a health warning because of his effect on my heart rate. He looked totally shocked which was a bit sobering.

Not all men had his attributes. Now and then a large man would stroll from the pool to the gym changing rooms.

For some the only way they could possibly see their willies was in a mirror, hitching their stomach up. There should have been a rule about keeping shirts on until inside the changing room.

Whilst I am not fanatical about it, I discovered to my dismay that the more I worked out the heavier I got. There's no justice! I'm told the reason is that fat weighs less than muscle. However if you stop exercising, all the muscles that have been built up, very quickly revert to fat, and with that comes flabby skin! So slow and steady rather than going for the burn every visit seemed to be the best plan. I am desperate to avoid chicken wings.

My other big bugbear is that, as result of a fat fuelled childhood, there is not a glimmer of light between my thighs. They are as though glued together. I also have a bum that many women would pay a lot to acquire. It seems the more exercise I do the bigger it gets. Anyway with regard to my thighs most gyms have a pair of machines that work on the adductor muscles (inner thighs for the uninitiated), and abductors, for the outer thighs. Now even with an induction session I nearly came a cropper on the former. To use this machine you sit on the seat and put your legs outside of two pads attached to adjustable weights. It's possible to adjust how wide you push your thighs apart and how much weight you attempt to push. When I first joined my current gym, much fitter than I am now during lockdown, I forced my thighs as far apart as possible, and then some. I set the weights at 35kgs and managed to do 80 pushes bringing the pads together most times. What I didn't know was that in order to release the paddles and allow dismounting I needed to stretch my thighs even further apart. Only then will the release mechanism work. I was stuck. I tried my best to look nonchalant. There was no way I could attract anyone's attention, they were all doing their own thing and wearing earphones that blocked out all extraneous sound. Panic set in. Finally, after what seemed an endless struggle with the release lever, I figured out that if I pressed really hard against the back of the seat and held on to it, I could wriggle my bum up far enough for my legs to slacken on the paddles. At last when I pulled the release lever, it worked and I was free. I sat there for some time to recover before venturing further.

I refused to be deterred by young, slim women who could wrap their legs around their necks. I tried not to get irritated by the friends, usually youngish women, who went around in pairs and talked endlessly about what they were cooking for dinner, where they're going on holiday etc. I still remember vividly one who described in minute detail how sick she was after a night on the town. I have always resisted earphones, purely because I can't figure out the technology of getting music onto the relevant bit of equipment. But maybe just earphones would be a good idea? What is lovely to see is women even older than me who look out for each other, check on how they're doing, all very quietly in a world of their own. I overheard a conversation where one lady said, 'Coming to the gym gave a structure to her week.' I totally get that.

Now about trainers – the human kind as opposed to what we put on our feet. I tried a woman first. She had me stretching things I really shouldn't have stretched. Thinking I had just pulled a muscle I decided to work through it. I used the rowing machine, attempted to run not walk on the treadmill, to no avail. My back and hip got so painful I wore the skin off one elbow because it was the only way I could ease myself out of bed. I got to one booking in London and thought I'd have to call for someone to help me get out of the car. I almost resorted to getting a stick and probably should have done. Thankfully my doctor, the same one who left me to faint for seven years, put it down to wearing one-inch heels (really), and noted, 'I was hobbling a bit', went on holiday. Her relief was a locum from the Nuffield Orthopaedic hospital. He recognised a damaged disk when he met one! That was the end to my rowing, and running (gently) on the treadmill. Happily with the exercises he gave me and the combination of painkillers and anti-inflammatory tablets my back improved.

COVID-19 has put an end to my visits to the gym. I am awaiting the delivery of a recumbent bike. Weights have already arrived. The local postman is quite a character. He put the box of 2 x 3kgs weights on the doorstep and said, 'Go on pick it up.' I did!!! All is not lost.

What next?

As for what the future holds, who knows? I'd like to keep on experiencing the pleasures, but not the heartaches, for as long as I can, and perhaps when I finally do head for that big bed in the sky, I can look back and smile on a life well lived, and lusted.

How would I like to go?

'Parker... harder, harder, I'm coming,' I moan.

Parker responds with a compliant, 'Yes, m'Lady,' and proceeds to increase the speed and force of his thrusting.

I then enjoy a long drawn out orgasm followed by a very quick cardiac arrest. I am 100 years old.

To Be Continued...

Published by

www.publishandprint.co.uk